My United States

Virginia

JENNIFER HACKETT

Children's Press®
An Imprint of Scholastic Inc.

Content Consultant

James Wolfinger, PhD, Associate Dean and Professor

College of Education, DePaul University, Chicago, Illinois

Library of Congress Cataloging-in-Publication Data
Names: Hackett, Jennifer, author.
Title: Virginia / by Jennifer Hackett.
Description: New York : Children's Press, an imprint of Scholastic Inc., 2018. | Series: A true book | Includes
    bibliographical references and index.
Identifiers: LCCN 2017025788 | ISBN 9780531231715 (library binding) | ISBN 9780531247228 (pbk.)
Subjects: LCSH: Virginia—Juvenile literature.
Classification: LCC F226.3 .H33 2018 | DDC 975.5—dc23
LC record available at https://lccn.loc.gov/2017025788

Photos ©: cover: Pat & Chuck Blackley/Alamy Images; back cover bottom: Digital Vision/Thinkstock; back cover ribbon: AliceLiddelle/Getty Images; 3 bottom: Americanspirit/Dreamstime; 3 map: Jim McMahon; 4 left: Alan Murphy/Minden Pictures/Superstock, Inc.; 4 right: ValentynVolkov/iStockphoto; 5 top: Hiroya Minakuchi/Minden Pictures/Superstock, Inc.; 5 bottom: John Henley/Media Bakery; 7 center bottom: Jorge Villalba/Dreamstime; 7 top: M Timothy O'Keefe/Getty Images; 7 bottom: Universal Images Group/Superstock, Inc.; 7 center top: traveler1116/iStockphoto; 8-9: tmersh/iStockphoto; 11: zrfphoto/iStockphoto; 12: Alex Potemkin/iStockphoto; 13: Joe Fudge/MCT/Newscom; 14: Hiroya Minakuchi/Minden Pictures/Superstock, Inc.; 15: Rob & Ann Simpson/Visuals Unlimited, Inc./Getty Images; 16-17: SeanPavonePhoto/iStockphoto; 19: Sarin Images/The Granger Collection; 20: Tigatelu/Dreamstime; 22 right: fckncg/Shutterstock; 22 left: Atlaspix/Shutterstock; 23 top left: Alan Murphy/Minden Pictures/Superstock, Inc.; 23 center left: Tracy Morgan/Getty Images; 23 top right: OGphoto/iStockphoto; 23 bottom right: ValentynVolkov/iStockphoto; 23 bottom left: Josie Iselin/Visuals Unlimited, Inc./Getty Images; 23 center right: eliasenova/iStockphoto; 24-25: World History Archive/Superstock, Inc.; 27: Marilyn Angel Wynn/Getty Images; 29: W. Langdon Kihn/National Geographic Creative/Alamy Images; 30 bottom: Everett Historical/Shutterstock; 30 top: Atlaspix/Shutterstock; 31 top left: North Wind Picture Archives; 31 bottom: North Wind Picture Archives; 31 top right: Francis Miller/The LIFE Picture Collection/Getty Images; 32: Mehmet Demirci/ZUMAPRESS/Newscom; 33: The Granger Collection; 34-35: Randy Duchaine/Alamy Images; 36: Joe Sargent/Getty Images; 37: Teresa Kenney/Dreamstime; 38: Andrew Harrer/Bloomberg/Getty Images; 39: Edwin Remsberg/age fotostock; 40 inset: Marie C Fields/Shutterstock; 40 bottom: PepitoPhotos/iStockphoto; 41: John Henley/Media Bakery; 42 right: Gilbert Stuart/Getty Images; 42 bottom left: ClassicStock.com/Superstock, Inc.; 42 center left: bauhaus1000/Getty Images; 42 top left: Culture Club/Getty Images; 43 bottom right: Robert Daemmrich Photography Inc/Corbis/Getty Images; 43 bottom center: Turkbug/Dreamstime; 43 center left: Everett Collection; 43 top right: Anthony Bruno/Michael Ochs Archives/Getty Images; 43 top left: Universal Images Group/Superstock, Inc.; 43 bottom left: Debby Wong/Shutterstock; 44 center: Nazlisart/Dreamstime; 44 bottom: Photri/Topham/The Image Works; 44 top left: Jon Edwards/Getty Images; 45 center left: Andre Jenny Stock Connection Worldwide/Newscom; 45 center right: kaanates/iStockphoto; 45 top: North Wind Picture Archives; 45 bottom: Sarin Images/The Granger Collection. Maps by Map Hero, Inc.

Scholastic Inc., 557 Broadway, New York, NY 10012

1 2 3 4 5 6 7 8 9 10 R 27 26 25 24 23 22 21 20 19 18

Front cover: A Virginia farm

Back cover: The Pentagon

Welcome to Virginia

Find the Truth!

Everything you are about to read is true *except* for one of the sentences on this page.

Which one is **TRUE**?

T or F Virginia was the first state to join the Union.

T or F More presidents have been born in Virginia than any other state.

Find the answers in this book.

Key Facts

Capital: Richmond

Estimated population as of 2016: 8,411,808

Nicknames: Old Dominion, Mother of Presidents

Biggest cities: Virginia Beach, Norfolk, Chesapeake

UNITED STATES

Virginia

VIRGINIA
MNGSUN
TIGER SWALLOWTAIL-
STATE INSECT

Contents

THE BIG TRUTH!

Oyster

What Represents Virginia?

Cardinal

Fall colors along the
Blue Ridge Parkway

3 History

4 Culture

Fishing in Virginia

5

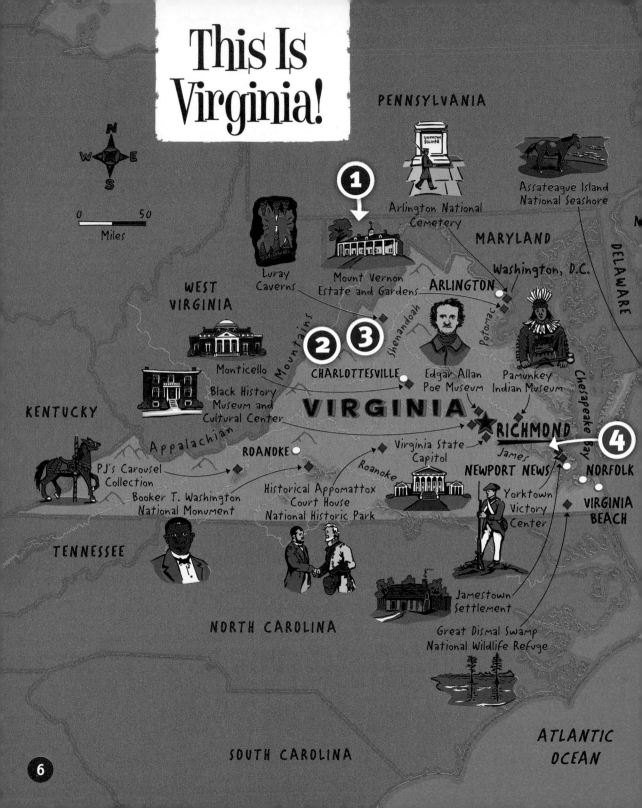

This Is Virginia!

PENNSYLVANIA

N
W E
S

0   50
Miles

① Arlington National Cemetery

Assateague Island National Seashore

Luray Caverns

Mount Vernon Estate and Gardens

ARLINGTON

Washington, D.C.

MARYLAND

DELAWARE

WEST VIRGINIA

Shenandoah

Potomac

Monticello

② ③ CHARLOTTESVILLE

Edgar Allan Poe Museum

Pamunkey Indian Museum

Mountains

Black History Museum and Cultural Center

VIRGINIA

Cherapeake Bay

KENTUCKY

Appalachian

RICHMOND

④

ROANOKE

Virginia State Capitol

James

NORFOLK

PJ's Carousel Collection

Booker T. Washington National Monument

Roanoke

NEWPORT NEWS

VIRGINIA BEACH

Historical Appomattox Court House National Historic Park

Yorktown Victory Center

TENNESSEE

Jamestown Settlement

NORTH CAROLINA

Great Dismal Swamp National Wildlife Refuge

SOUTH CAROLINA

ATLANTIC OCEAN

① Mount Vernon

George Washington's estate in northern Virginia started as a farmhouse built in 1735. Washington built it into an impressive **plantation** with a mansion that still stands today.

② American Shakespeare Center and Blackfriars Playhouse

The Blackfriars Playhouse is the only re-creation of Blackfriars Theater in London, England. The London theater was where some of William Shakespeare's plays were originally performed.

③ Luray Caverns

These natural caverns in the Shenandoah Valley were discovered in 1878. Inside is the Great Stalacpipe Organ. This system of rubber mallets hits 37 different naturally formed **stalactites** to make music.

④ Busch Gardens

Busch Gardens Williamsburg has several different areas inspired by European countries. Each one has rides, food, and more.

Virginia has 3,315 miles (5,335 kilometers) of ocean coastline.

CHAPTER 1

Land and Wildlife

Smack in the middle of the East Coast, Virginia is full of sandy beaches, green mountains, and scenic countryside. Rushing rivers flow through it, and its coast boasts many natural **harbors**. In some ways, it is a "Goldilocks" state. It isn't one of the biggest, but it isn't one of the smallest either. It doesn't get very hot, but it also doesn't get very cold. Maybe that's why Virginia has attracted so many residents that it has the 12th-largest population in the United States!

From the Mountains to the Coast

Virginia is full of tree-covered mountains. The western part of the state has 544 miles (875 km) of the 2,200-mile-long (3,541 km) Appalachian Trail—a bigger piece than any other state. It also has many major rivers, which help make the farmland throughout most of the state fertile. These include the Potomac, Shenandoah, James, Rappahannock, and York Rivers. They all flow into the Chesapeake Bay, the largest **estuary** in North America.

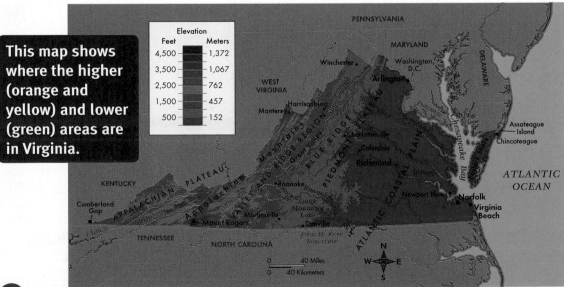

This map shows where the higher (orange and yellow) and lower (green) areas are in Virginia.

Shenandoah Valley

The Shenandoah Valley lies between the Blue Ridge Mountains and the Valley and Ridge area of the Appalachians. It gets its name from the Shenandoah River, which flows along most of the length of the valley. The valley is full of waterfalls and quiet wooded areas. Songbirds and deer make its 200,000 acres (80,937 hectares) of protected land home. Its fertile soil is home to apple orchards and lavender fields. The valley also has 500 miles (805 km) of hiking trails. This makes it perfect for a day trip to explore nature.

Grazing cattle are a common sight on the farms of the Piedmont. Virginia's dairy cows produce more than 205 million gallons (776 million liters) of milk each year.

The eastern part of Virginia lies along the Atlantic Ocean. It has many sandy beaches and harbors, including Hampton Roads. Hampton Roads is one of the largest natural harbors in the world and is ice-free year-round.

Much of Virginia lies in the Piedmont, a **plateau** region that runs through the central part of the state. This area's fertile, clay-like soil is perfect for growing crops such as corn and apples.

Mild and Wild Weather

Virginia has a mild and pleasant climate. Most of the state is between 30 and 40 degrees Fahrenheit (–1 and 4 degrees Celsius) in the winter and 60° and 88°F (15° and 31°C) in the summer. Most snowfall is in the mountains in the west and southwest, where temperatures are usually cooler. Sometimes Virginia has **severe** weather, like heavy rainfall caused by hurricanes. The state gets rain about 100 days every year.

MAXIMUM TEMPERATURE
110° F

MINIMUM TEMPERATURE
-30° F

In 2012, Superstorm Sandy brought massive floods to many parts of Virginia. People had to use boats to get around.

HIGH WATER

Full of Forests

Almost two-thirds of Virginia is covered in forests. The state has an amazing variety of trees. There are pines, cedars, willows, hickories, poplars, oaks, elms, sycamores, maples, ashes, and more. Oaks and pines make up most of the forests. Thousands of other plants are native to Virginia. The Virginia creeper and common wood sorrel are found across the state. Other plants, like the Mattaponi quillwort, are only found in a few counties.

In fall, Virginia's trees turn a wide variety of colors.

A salamander crawls through Shenandoah National Park in Virginia.

Amazing Animals

Animals big and small make Virginia their home. The state's mountains and forests are filled with black bears, bobcats, and white-tailed deer. They're also home to the Shenandoah salamander, which is found only in Virginia. Snakes and lizards slither throughout the state.

The water is full of aquatic life. Fish such as trout and striped bass swim through the rivers, while whales and dolphins can be spotted along Virginia's ocean shores. Many people travel to the state's beaches in hope of glimpsing one of these amazing creatures.

Richmond is Virginia's state capital, and it was the capital of the entire Confederacy during the Civil War.

CHAPTER 2

Government

When British settlers first came to Virginia in 1607, they settled in Jamestown. Jamestown was the center of Virginia's government until 1699, when it was replaced by Williamsburg. After Virginia and the other American **colonies** declared independence from Great Britain in 1776, Williamsburg became the capital of the new state. Four years later, in 1780, the state capital was moved to Richmond, where it has remained ever since.

The Branches of Government

Virginia's government is divided into three branches. The governor leads the executive branch, which enforces the state's laws. The General Assembly, made up of a House of Delegates and a Senate, serves as the state's legislative branch. Its 140 members are responsible for writing laws. The judicial branch, made up of the state's courts, interprets and upholds these laws.

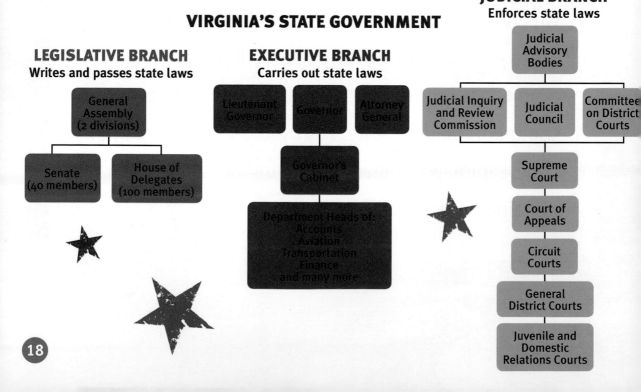

VIRGINIA'S STATE GOVERNMENT

LEGISLATIVE BRANCH
Writes and passes state laws

General Assembly (2 divisions)
- Senate (40 members)
- House of Delegates (100 members)

EXECUTIVE BRANCH
Carries out state laws

Lieutenant Governor · Governor · Attorney General

Governor's Cabinet

Department Heads of: Accounts, Aviation, Transportation, Finance, and many more

JUDICIAL BRANCH
Enforces state laws

Judicial Advisory Bodies
- Judicial Inquiry and Review Commission
- Judicial Council
- Committee on District Courts

Supreme Court

Court of Appeals

Circuit Courts

General District Courts

Juvenile and Domestic Relations Courts

The First American Legislature

Founded in 1619, Virginia's House of Burgesses was the first legislative body in the American colonies. It was made up of the Virginia General Assembly, which still meets today and is the oldest legislature in North America. This body helped inspire the legislative branch for the entire United States. Many Founding Fathers, including Thomas Jefferson, George Washington, and Patrick Henry, served in the House of Burgesses at some point.

Patrick Henry speaks out about a British tax at the Virginia House of Burgesses in 1765.

Virginia in the National Government

Each state elects officials to represent it in the U.S. Congress. Like every state, Virginia has two senators. The U.S. House of Representatives relies on a state's population to determine its numbers. Virginia has 11 representatives in the House.

Every four years, states vote on the next U.S. president. Each state is granted a number of electoral votes based on its number of members of Congress. With two senators and 11 representatives, Virginia has 13 electoral votes.

2 senators and 11 representatives

13 electoral votes

Virginia has an above-average number of electoral votes.

The People of Virginia

Elected officials in Virginia represent a population with a range of interests, lifestyles, and backgrounds.

Ethnicity (2016 estimates)

19.8%
African American

62.4%
Caucasian

9.1%
Hispanic or Latino

0.5%
Native American or Alaska Native

6.6%
Asian

0.1%
Native Hawaiian or other Pacific Islander

2.9%
Two or more races

More than
700,000
Virginians are military veterans.

66%
own their homes.

36.3%
of Virginians have graduated from college.

15.4%
speak a language other than English at home.

88.3%
of the population graduated from high school.

11.7%
of Virginians were born in other countries.

21

What Represents Virginia?

States choose specific animals, plants, and objects to represent the values and characteristics of the land and its people. Find out why these symbols were chosen to represent Virginia or discover surprising curiosities about them.

Seal

The state seal depicts a figure representing virtue standing atop another figure representing tyranny. This symbolizes the American victory over Great Britain in the Revolutionary War.

Flag

Virginia's state flag simply displays the state seal against a blue field.

Cardinal

STATE BIRD

Unlike many birds, both male and female cardinals can sing.

Dogwood

STATE FLOWER

Thomas Jefferson grew this flower at his Virginia estate, Monticello.

American Foxhound

STATE DOG

This hunting dog was first bred in Virginia in the 1700s.

Milk

STATE BEVERAGE

Virginia is home to about 90,000 dairy cows.

Chesapecten jeffersonius

STATE FOSSIL

This fossil comes from the shell of an ancient scallop.

Oyster Shell

STATE SHELL

Oyster shells can be seen washed up on Virginia's beaches.

More than 2,000 battles were fought in Virginia during the Civil War.

CHAPTER 3

History

There was some confusion when English settlers first explored what would become Virginia. Scouts told Queen Elizabeth I, England's ruler at the time, that a Native American man named Wingina was the king of a land called Wingandacoa. The next voyage's translator revealed that the earlier settlers had misunderstood. *Wingandacoa* actually meant "What good clothes you wear!"

Native Americans

Native Americans have lived in Virginia for more than 12,000 years. An estimated 50,000 Native Americans lived there when European colonization began. There were three major groups, with each speaking a different language. People who spoke Algonquian lived along the coast. Those who spoke Iroquois lived in the south. Sioux speakers lived in Virginia's central region.

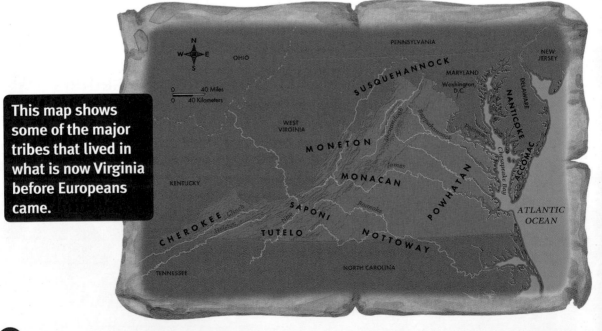

This map shows some of the major tribes that lived in what is now Virginia before Europeans came.

Some Powhatan people built homes by stretching animal skins and other materials over wooden frames.

One major group of Native Americans was the Powhatan. The Powhatan were made up of about 30 Algonquian-speaking tribes. By the 1600s, about 22,000 Powhatan people lived in villages along the coast. Villages consisted of several large buildings often surrounded by a protective fence. In nearby fields, Powhatan farmers grew beans, corn, and other crops. The Powhatan also hunted animals for meat and skins.

New Arrivals

Virginia was first spotted by Spanish explorers in the 1500s. English settlers tried to establish a colony in the 1580s, but they weren't successful. The Virginia Company was created by King James I of Great Britain in 1606 to establish settlements in North America. The British wanted to look for gold and valuable materials to send back to England. In 1607, the Virginia Company started a settlement called Jamestown.

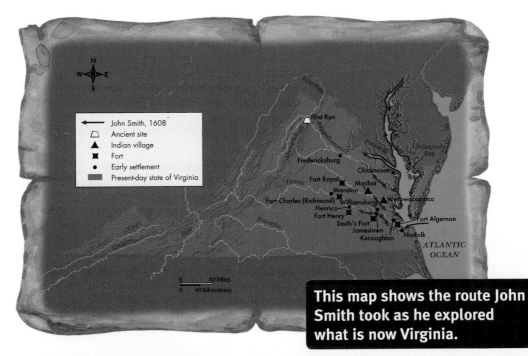

This map shows the route John Smith took as he explored what is now Virginia.

Matoaka, better known as Pocahontas, was a young Powhatan girl who became friendly with the Jamestown settlers.

Early British settlers had a difficult time. They first relied on help from the Paspahegh tribe, who were part of the Powhatan. Still, many settlers died of hunger. Settlers had also brought diseases, such as smallpox, and started many conflicts with Native Americans. Both of these resulted in the deaths of many Native Americans. Jamestown was able to survive with help from Great Britain. More settlements, including Williamsburg, were soon established throughout Virginia.

A New Country

As one of the first British colonies, Virginia played a big part in the creation of the United States. It was one of the 13 original colonies that declared independence from British rule in 1776. It was also the site of the last battle of the Revolutionary War: the Battle of Yorktown. After the war, Virginia became the 10th state to join the Union when it ratified the U.S. Constitution in June 1788.

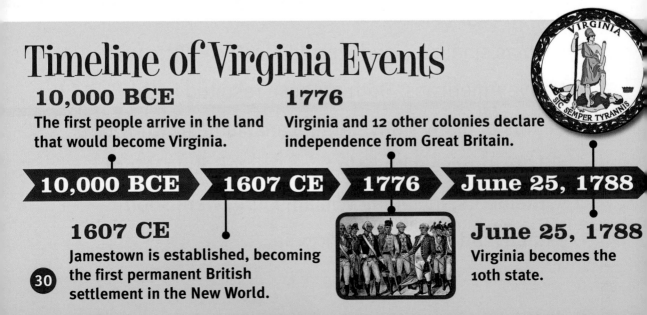

Timeline of Virginia Events

10,000 BCE
The first people arrive in the land that would become Virginia.

1776
Virginia and 12 other colonies declare independence from Great Britain.

| 10,000 BCE | 1607 CE | 1776 | June 25, 1788 |

1607 CE
Jamestown is established, becoming the first permanent British settlement in the New World.

June 25, 1788
Virginia becomes the 10th state.

The Civil War

Virginia had many plantations that grew tobacco and cotton. To work these plantations, most Virginians had slaves. Slavery was supported by the Southern states and opposed by the Northern states. Virginia joined the South in **seceding** from the Union in May 1861, and Richmond became the capital of the Confederacy. Most of the fighting during the Civil War took place in Virginia. At the end of the war in 1865, fleeing Confederates set Richmond on fire, but the arriving Union army saved the city from destruction.

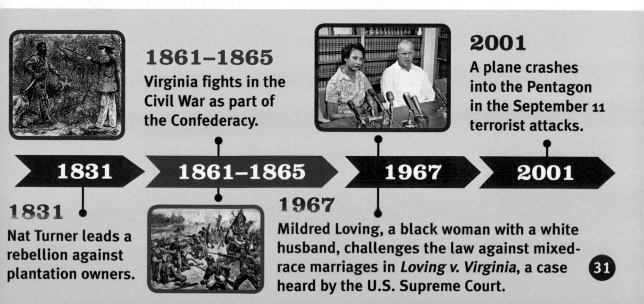

1861–1865
Virginia fights in the Civil War as part of the Confederacy.

2001
A plane crashes into the Pentagon in the September 11 terrorist attacks.

| 1831 | 1861–1865 | 1967 | 2001 |

1831
Nat Turner leads a rebellion against plantation owners.

1967
Mildred Loving, a black woman with a white husband, challenges the law against mixed-race marriages in *Loving v. Virginia*, a case heard by the U.S. Supreme Court.

U.S. Marines train at their base in Quantico, Virginia.

Close to the Capital

Part of Virginia was used to create Washington, D.C., in 1790. This became the new nation's capital. Many politicians and government leaders made their homes in Virginia because it was so close to the capital. This is still the case today, as many people involved in governing the nation live in northern Virginia. The area is also home to many people who serve in the country's military.

Maggie L. Walker

Maggie L. Walker was born Maggie Lena Mitchell on July 15, 1864, during the Civil War. She was the daughter of a former slave. From the age of 16, Walker worked as part of the Independent Order of St. Luke, an organization that helped the sick and elderly and supported African Americans. She became the first woman in the United States to found a bank when she opened St. Luke Penny Savings Bank in 1903. Walker used her wealth and intelligence to help other African Americans. She also advocated for disabled people.

Norfolk has 17 mermaid statues on display. Each is roughly 10 feet (3 meters) long.

CHAPTER 4

Culture

Virginia supports all kinds of art, from stage to canvas. The first Friday of every month is a celebration of art in Richmond. Colorful mermaids painted by local artists are scattered around Norfolk. Performing arts are a large part of Virginia's culture. The state is home to many theaters where plays, dance pieces, and other shows are performed. Authors such as Edgar Allan Poe have also called the state home.

Sports and Recreation

Many hikers visit Virginia to explore the state's many mountains and trails. Canoeing or kayaking on the James River is a popular summer pastime for locals and visitors alike.

There are no professional sports teams in Virginia, but the state's many universities are well known for their teams. Virginians love rooting for Virginia Commonwealth University's basketball team and the Virginia Tech Hokies football team.

Exciting Events

Virginia's festivals celebrate the state's history, food, and culture. The Shenandoah Apple Blossom Festival shows off Winchester's beautiful valley. It has parades, dances, a race, and more. On the coast, the Chincoteague Pony Swim highlights the wild horses that swim between two islands. The horses have been doing this for almost 100 years! Other events in the state celebrate everything from local produce to music. There's even an annual hot-air balloon rally!

Members of the Jaffa Motor Corps drive small cars in the Apple Blossom Festival's Grand Feature Parade.

Workers conduct tests on equipment aboard an aircraft carrier in Newport News.

Off to Work

Because Virginia is so close to the nation's capital, it is home to many politicians, experts on foreign countries, and even FBI agents. Engineering is also a major occupation in Virginia. Some engineers work on ships, while others work on planes or even nuclear reactors. There are also many captains and sailors. They might work as fishers or sail on historical tall ships.

Advances in Agriculture

Farmers have lived in Virginia for hundreds of years. Farming is still a major **industry** in the state. The earliest cash crops in Virginia were tobacco, cotton, and corn. Founding Fathers such as Thomas Jefferson and George Washington planted these crops on their farms. Today, there are almost 45,000 farms across the state. More than 440,000 people work on them. Soybeans, apples, grapes, tomatoes, and peanuts are just a few of the foods these farmers grow. Unlike the early settlers in the state, today's farmers can use huge, powerful machines to plants and harvest large fields.

A Virginia farmer stands near his soybean harvester.

Time to Eat

Virginia is known for its ham, peanuts, and seafood. One town, Smithfield, is famous for its smoked ham. Wakefield's Virginia Diner sends its special peanuts all over the country. Along the coast, people love to eat fresh oysters and blue crabs. Apples and other tasty fruits are also grown all over Virginia.

★ ★ Virginia Ham Biscuits

Ask an adult to help you!

This recipe was a favorite of Martha Washington!

Ingredients

Butter
2 cups all-purpose flour plus extra for dusting
2 teaspoons baking powder
1 teaspoon salt

1/4 cup cold lard, cut into small pieces
1 cup milk plus extra for brushing
Thin slices of Virginia ham or some other filling

Directions

Preheat an oven to 450 degrees. Butter a baking sheet. Mix together the flour, baking powder, and salt in a large bowl. Add the lard and, using a fork, cut it into the mixture until it looks like coarse crumbs. Add the milk and stir until the mixture makes a soft dough. Form the dough into a ball. Dust a clean surface with flour. Roll the dough out until it's about 1/2 inch thick. Use a 1-inch cookie cutter to make circles. Transfer the circles to the baking sheet and brush the tops with milk. Bake the biscuits for 10 to 12 minutes until golden. Let cool, then fill them with ham or your favorite filling!

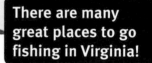

There are many great places to go fishing in Virginia!

A Remarkable Place to Be

Virginia is jam-packed with fun and adventure. Its mild climate, beautiful environment, and mix of cultures mean there's always something to do or see. As one of the first 13 states, the history of Virginia is also the history of the country itself. It's no wonder more presidents have been born in Virginia than any other state! ★

Famous People

Pocahontas

(1596?–1617) was a Powhatan woman believed to have saved the life of John Smith, a British settler and leader of the Jamestown settlement.

George Washington

(1732–1799) was an American Revolution military leader who became the first president of the United States. He was born in Virginia to a family of tobacco plantation owners.

Patrick Henry

(1736–1799) was one of the country's Founding Fathers. He served as the first and sixth governor of Virginia.

Thomas Jefferson

(1743–1826) was the third president of the United States and the author of the Declaration of Independence. He was a Virginia resident for most of his life.

Edgar Allan Poe

(1809–1849) was a writer known for poems such as "The Raven" and stories such as "The Tell-Tale Heart." He attended the University of Virginia and spent most of his life in the state.

Ella Fitzgerald

(1917–1996) was a jazz singer known as the First Lady of Song. She was born in Newport News.

Arthur Ashe

(1943–1993) was the first and only African American man to win the singles competition in tennis at Wimbledon, the U.S. Open, and the Australian Open. He was born in Richmond.

Gabby Douglas

(1995–) is a gymnast from Newport News who was part of the U.S. Olympic teams in 2012 and 2016. She won three Olympic gold medals in 2012.

Katie Couric

(1957–) is a journalist who has hosted or co-hosted shows on ABC, CBS, and NBC, including NBC's *Today Show*. She was born in Arlington.

Pharrell Williams

(1973–) is a multiple Grammy Award–winning musician and producer known for songs such as "Happy." He was born in Virginia Beach.

43

Did You Know That . . .

The first Thanksgiving in North America was celebrated in Virginia in 1619.

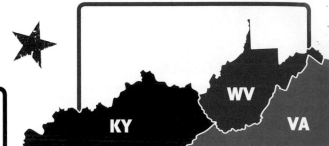

Both Kentucky and West Virginia were formed from parts of the original state of Virginia.

Eight presidents were born in Virginia. That is more than any other state! These presidents were George Washington, Thomas Jefferson, James Madison, James Monroe, William Harrison, John Tyler, Zachary Taylor, and Woodrow Wilson.

The Pentagon in Arlington is one of the largest office buildings in the world. It has 68,000 miles (109,435 km) of internal telephone lines!

The College of William and Mary in Williamsburg is the second-oldest college in the United States. It was founded in 1693. Its Wren Hall is the oldest continuously used academic building in the country.

About one-half of all the battles in the Civil War were fought in Virginia.

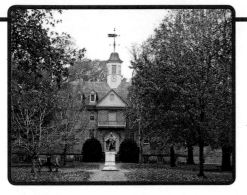

The country's first peanut crops were grown in Virginia.

18%

About 18 percent of Virginia's residents work for the U.S. government.

Did you find the truth?

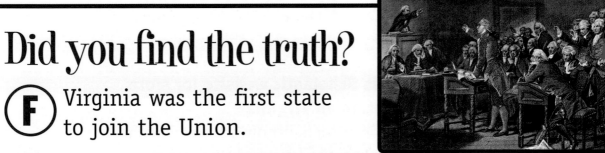

(F) Virginia was the first state to join the Union.

(T) More presidents have been born in Virginia than any other state.

Resources

Books

Nonfiction

De Angelis, Gina. *Virginia*. New York: Children's Press, 2009.

Kent, Deborah. *Virginia*. New York: Children's Press, 2014.

Fiction

Henry, Marguerite. *Misty of Chincoteague*. Chicago: Rand McNally, 1947.

Paterson, Katherine. *The Great Gilly Hopkins*. New York: Crowell, 1978.

Important Words

colonies (KAH-luh-neez) settlements formed by people from a foreign country

estuary (ES-choo-er-ee) the wide part of a river's lower end, where it meets the sea

harbors (HAR-burz) safe areas of water where boats can be anchored

industry (IN-duh-stree) a type of business that employs a large number of people

plantation (plan-TAY-shuhn) a large farm or estate used for growing tobacco, cotton, or other crops to sell

plateau (pla-TOH) a high, level area of land

seceding (suh-SEED-ing) withdrawing from a group or a political union

severe (suh-VEER) very strong or intense

stalactites (stuh-LAK-tites) pointed structures that hang from the roofs of caves

Index

Page numbers in **bold** indicate illustrations.

About the Author

Jennifer Hackett studied physics and history at the College of William and Mary—which means she spent a lot of time in Virginia! After she decided she wanted to write instead of research, she attended New York University's Science, Health, and Environmental Reporting Program. She currently works as Scholastic MATH's associate editor. Colonial Williamsburg and Busch Gardens are two of her favorite places in Virginia. (Her favorite roller coaster is Apollo's Chariot!)